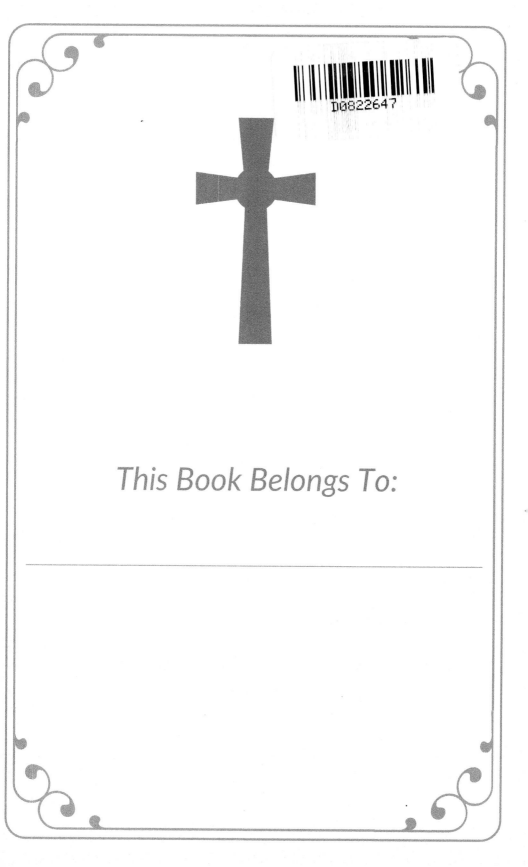

This Book Belongs To:

Saint Augustine

1 Chronicles 16:8

Oh, give thanks to the Lord; call upon his name; make known his deeds among the peoples! (ESV).

As Christians, sharing our testimony is second-nature. We long to tell the world of the marvelous things that Christ has done in our lives! Out of the abundance God has given us, we want to share with others. We live out our lives grateful for the way the Lord has reached into our hearts, and we desire for others to experience the same.

Saint Augustine of Hippo lead by example and inspired generations of believers to share their stories openly. His work, Confessions, details his journey from hedonism to faith. Back when he wrote it, it was more common to see works on theology than personal testimonies. His boldness in sharing and the vulnerability he displayed influenced so many for the cause of Christ.

Who have you shared your story with? Our experiences hold the power to alter the course of another's life drastically. God calls us to be open in our faith and make known to the world how He has impacted our lives. Our testimonies should flow my our lips out of a place of grateful abundance as we live in His love.

Your faith has likely been influenced by the story of another as well. Consider for a moment where you'd be if that person weren't so willing to share with you. Your own experiences are unique, and you never know who needs to hear what you have to say. Pray that God would direct you to those who would be inspired by your story and that the Holy Spirit would be evident through your words.

Reflections

_____
_____
_____
_____
_____
_____

Prayers

_____
_____
_____
_____
_____
_____
_____

Saint Katharine Drexel

Philippians 2:3

Do nothing from selfish ambition or conceit, but in humility count others more significant than yourselves (ESV).

In response to God's love, our hearts are filled with selfless devotion. The life of a believer is one of serving others, following in the example that Jesus showed us. Saint Katharine Drexel blazed a trail of selfless devotion that can serve as a powerful illustration to us today. The Holy Spirit was made manifest through her servant's heart.

Always loving the Lord, Saint Katharine chose a life solely devoted to God instead of a husband. All she wanted to do was serve the Lord and others. Her missional journey led to her serving Indian populations in the American West, a place that God was putting on her heart to help. This mission culminated in the creation of the Sisters of the Blessed Sacrament, an order devoted to establishing missions and schools for American Indians and African Americans. Even after suffering health complications that left her virtually immobile, her devotion to the Lord didn't cease. Though she could no longer enter the missionary field, she spent the last twenty years of her life selflessly devoted to prayer.

God likewise calls us to a life of service. He has given us each unique gifts that will allow us to serve His Kingdom in an impactful way. We must be laser-focused on cultivating our gifts and putting them into practice for the sake of those who need us. We can be the hands of Jesus in this world, spreading His love and healing to everyone. This opportunity is an immeasurable honor and responsibility that we should be grateful to accept. Ask God through prayer how He would use you for His Kingdom today.

Reflections

_____
_____
_____
_____
_____
_____
_____

Prayers

_____
_____
_____
_____
_____
_____
_____

Saint Irene

Sometimes God uses our experiences to change our lives. We may be going down a path utterly separate from His love when suddenly, we encounter something that changes our ways. This catalyst can be a person that inspires us, an event that shocks us, or a thing that opens our eyes to the truth. God can take any experience, good or bad, and turn it into an opportunity to reach into our lives.

That's precisely what happened to St. Irene. She grew up a pagan, but as a young woman, she broke up a shocking act of violence that disgusted her. The man she saved recovered and brought her to faith in God. She went on to live a life of devout Christian faith and service to others.

God altered the course of St. Irene's life through this horrible event she witnessed. He rewarded her compassionate heart with salvation in Him. God wants to use your circumstances to lead you to Him as well. How will you respond when He calls you to action? The choice you make can change your life.

Romans 8:28 reads,

"And we know that in all things God works for the good of those who love him" (NIV).

It's not only the good things that God puts in our path to draw us to Him. Even when confronted with a challenging situation, look for God within it and what He might be saying to you. Surely you will find Him there, and He will reach into your heart in a powerful way

Reflections

Prayers

Blessed Tomasa Ortiz Real

Children are one of our greatest blessings from the Lord. God blesses us richly when He shares with us what only He previously was capable of doing: bring forth new life. Bringing children into this world and raising them in the Lord is a way that we emulate Him. We have a great responsibility in bringing up the next generation of God's children.

Blessed Tomasa Ortiz Real lived her life in service of ill and orphaned children. She took Jesus' words seriously when He said,

"Whoever welcomes one such child in my name welcomes me"
(Matt. 18:5, NIV).

God put a calling on her heart, and she responded in kind. She is an excellent example for us all.

How do you treat the most vulnerable people in your life? Jesus bids us to welcome them and care for them as if we were serving Him. He likewise says that if we deny them anything they need which we can provide, that we also deny Him. If we want to experience the life-altering presence of Christ in our lives, we must serve as He did. We are His hands and feet in the world, and we must take that responsibility with the utmost seriousness.

Ask God to reach into your heart and renew your passion for meeting the needs of others. If you do, He will place a calling on your life that will lead you to work that will impact the world for His Kingdom. Let Blessed Tomasa Ortiz Real serve as an illustration of what God can do through us when we open our hearts to others' needs.

Reflections

Prayers

Blessed Artemide Zatti

God will often inspire us towards a particular calling in life in light of our own experiences. Sometimes we face things in life that move us towards helping others who are going through something similar. Sometimes our most influential work in ministry is the result of reaching into someone's life the way that no one else can because of shared experiences. People need to know that they are not alone in their struggles.

We can look towards Blessed Artemide Zatti as a beautiful example of this type of ministry in action. Faced with Tuberculosis, he was told that he had little hope for survival. He prayed, promising the dedication of his life to caring for the sick if he was healed. God answered his prayers and delivered him. Blessed Artemide Zatti was true to his promise, working in the San Jose pharmacy and hospital. The hospital is now named in his honor.

Blessed Artemide Zatti has touched many lives. He served those who were sick in their darkest hour, and he inspired so many Christians after him to follow in his footsteps. Jesus tells us that when we serve others, we are serving Him. Blessed Artemide Zatti served Jesus well.

Psalm 34:4 reads:
"I sought the LORD, and he answered me" (NIV).

How has God answered your prayers? Consider your answer to this question, praying to God and asking Him how your answer can be used to inspire others for the faith. Your life experiences can change the life of others. They can be your greatest asset in ministering to those in need. Ask that God would show you how in a powerful way.

Reflections

_____

_____

_____

_____

_____

_____

Prayers

_____

_____

_____

_____

_____

_____

Blessed Villana de'Botti

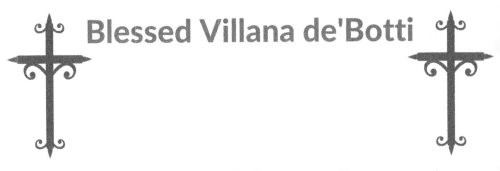

The world loves to tempt us with pleasures, pulling us away from our God-given purpose. God desires us to live a life of faith, but the enemy would see us walk in sin. We must stay diligent in remembering that the path of faith leads to salvation while that of sin sends us to destruction.

Blessed Villana de'Botti experienced this struggle in her life. Married off at a young age, she became intoxicated by the pleasures of life. This pattern continued until she couldn't even stand to accept the person she had become. She knew that she needed to make a change. She became a Dominican tertiary, devoting her life to prayer and reading God's Word.

How often do we find ourselves in the same challenging circumstances that Blessed Villana de'Botti found herself in? We earnestly seek to be a good person, even a good Christian, but the temptations of life distract. In an attempt to fill the voids within us with everything except for God, we lose ourselves in the process. We wake up one day, not even recognizing the person we have become.

Romans 12:2 reads,
"Do not conform to the pattern of this world, but be transformed by the renewing of your mind. Then you will be able to test and approve what God's will is--his good, pleasing and perfect will" (NIV).

God wants to enter into your life daily and show you the path to renewal. Commit to spending time with Him every day. He will not leave you alone in the struggles that you face. He will deliver you, for He is mightier than all sin.

Reflections

_____

_____

_____

_____

_____

_____

_____

Prayers

_____

_____

_____

_____

_____

_____

Saint David of Wales

God works through people like you and me to bring unbelievers to faith. He longs for all of us to influence others for the cause of the Gospel. How to respond to His call will determine your success in this endeavor. Never forget that your obedience to God's will for your life is tied to the future of another. You never know who will hear the message God has sent for you to share and how their entire life may be impacted as a result.

Saint David of Wales responded to God's calling on his life. His work for the Lord reaped a great reward, bring numerous people to the faith who had never known the Lord before. After receiving a vision from God, Saint David of Wales traveled to Jerusalem, preaching the Word and bringing many to salvation. He trusted in the Lord and went willingly where God sent him.

Where is God calling you? Have you responded to that call? You can trust God fully and completely, knowing that He has authority over all and wishes nothing but the best for your life. You can respond to His calling with full confidence that He will lead you precisely where you need to be. He wants to guide you in everything, making you a vessel through which His powerful work will come to fruition.

You have something special within you to offer the world. God desires to draw it out. He can utilize your unique skill set and talents in order to reach the world for Jesus.

Galatians 5:15 commands us to **_walk by the Spirit_** (NIV).

God wants to come into your life and show you where to go, if only you will let Him.

Reflections

Prayers

Saint Therese of Lisieux

God can call us to faith at any age. We must be ready and willing to accept that calling when it arrives. The Lord has given us so much, and we must be willing to respond in kind. Jesus sacrificed Himself on the cross for us, so the least we can do is obey when He speaks into our lives.

Saint Therese of Lisieux received a calling from God at the tender age of 15. Even at such a young age when life can be confusing and easy to be rebellious, Saint Therese listened, joining a Carmelite convent. The following statement became her motto:

"What matters in life is not great deeds, but great love."

Her gentle eagerness has inspired many to follow God wherever He may lead.

Where does God want you to be? Has He revealed a particular calling in your life? If so, are you walking on that path? If not, are you ready to accept it, no matter what it may be? These are the questions we must ask ourselves, no matter what step of our spiritual journey we may be on. If you need added motivation to do God's will, the story of Saint Therese of Lisieux provides an inspiring story of a young girl willing to trust God with all her heart.

We likewise need to trust Him in every aspect of our lives. He will never lead us astray. God knows the exact place that we will strive in Kingdom work, and He wants us to be there. Spend time with the Lord, prepare for His call, and be ready to answer when He calls. In doing this, you will please your Father in heaven.

Reflections

_____
_____
_____
_____
_____
_____
_____

Prayers

_____
_____
_____
_____
_____
_____
_____

Saint Casimir

When we live in devotion to Him, God grants us the ability to do things we could never have imagined before. We find out we have talents we never knew we had, and our capability to empathize with others' pain is increased beyond our comprehension. Not only does He open our hearts, motivating us to meet other's needs, but He equips us to do so. We carry His love with us as we go, spreading the message of the Gospel as we serve people.

Saint Casimir personified devotion to God and generosity towards those in need. He is the Patron Saint of Poland and Lithuania, with over 50 churches named after him. He is known for a mighty miracle that he performed through God's power during the Siege of Polotsk in 1518. He was able to show the Lithuanian troops where they could safely cross the Daugava River to save the city.

Saint Casimir trusted God and the gifts that He had bestowed on Him. When we show God the same trust, we, too, can experience a new side of us that God wants to pull out from within us. As we spend more and more time in His presence, we will grow little by little into the person we were created to be. When we do this, we will be ready to walk in the footsteps of Saints like Saint Casimir and do the work God has laid before us.

Are you ready to step up for God? Do you want to make a real impact on our world for the glory of God? If you said yes, I urge you to strive in everything you do to live a life of devotion to the Lord.

Reflections

_____
_____
_____
_____
_____
_____
_____

Prayers

_____
_____
_____
_____
_____
_____
_____

Saint Colette

Spiritual disciples have the unmatched ability in our lives to draw us deeper into our faith.

A healthy understanding of God's Word, coupled with a vibrant prayer life, are the building blocks of walking the Christian path. Devoting our time to such things will help us to stand stronger in our faith and face whatever the day may bring us.

Saint Colette was a remarkable example of how the spiritual disciplines can keep us focused on our faith. She was known to fast every Friday while meditating on Christ's Passion. The relationship she built with God inspired her to establish 17 convents and live a life of service to others. Through her meditation and prayer, God granted her visions that set her on a path of purpose.

No matter how busy we get, we must make time to do the things that please God. We must never stop striving to know Him more and more. There's no better way to do that than following in the footsteps of Saint Colette and devoting regular time to a practice that will inspire us for the sake of Christ.

John 17:3 reads:
"Now this is eternal life: that they know you, the only true God, and Jesus Christ, whom you have sent" (NIV).

If we know God and walk in His ways, we will have eternal life. That is exactly what God desires for us. Never lose sight of the goal. Avoid the pitfall of putting things that are temporary above things that will last forever.

Reflections

Prayers

Saint Oscar Arnulfo Romero y Galdamez

Following Jesus is the greatest thing that we can do in life. But with those benefits come great sacrifice. Just as Jesus bore His cross, to follow Him, we must take up ours as well. Following Christ means walking in His footsteps. The road He walked was perilous indeed, but what He accomplished changed the world. So too, can we impact the world through the work we do for Christ, no matter how difficult it may be.

Saint Oscar Arnulfo Romero y Galdámez saw out his devotion to Christ to the very end. He was ordained and appointed as a parish priest to a village in El Salvador in 1943 but rose to the rank of Arch Bishop of San Salvador. He spoke out for the poor and oppressed, social injustice, assassinations, and torture. In 1980, he was shot by a government-affiliated death squad while celebrating Mass in the chapel of La Divina Providencia Hospital in San Salvador, El Salvador.

2 Corinthians 1:7 reads:
"our hope for you is firmly grounded, knowing that as you are sharers of our sufferings, so also you are sharers of our comfort" (NIV).

As he wrote this verse, Paul was suffering many things for the cause of the Gospel as well. He wanted to remind us of the comfort God bestows upon us, even in our most significant challenges. Paul continued on in his ministry to the very end, likewise being murdered because of his boldness in preaching Christ.

Let us never think of ourselves too highly to commit to anything less than our all when devoting ourselves to Christ. Jesus gave His life for us, and no matter how hard it may be, we must be willing to do the same for Him.

Reflections

Prayers

Saint Vincent de Paul

When faced with challenging times in life, we have a choice to make. We can either complain and choose to live in our frustrations, or we can rise above our circumstances and live a life of impact. God empowers us to take our most challenging struggles and turn them into something beautiful.

That's precisely what Saint Vincent de Paul did. He lived a life of poverty and struggle, yet gave of himself to help others who were poor and destitute. He thought of others above himself and lived his life in service to them. He was a prime example to us all of what it means to meet other people's needs before our own.

Mark 10:45 reads:
"For even the Son of Man did not come to be served, but to serve, and to give his life as a ransom for many" (NIV).

If Jesus Himself, the only one worthy of honor and praise, came as a suffering servant, why should we try to take a higher place? We must follow in His example, doing every we can to help those who need us most.

If we do this in the name of Jesus, we will be spreading God's love as we do His work. Ministering to others opens up the door to talking with others about Christ and setting them on the path to salvation. It is a great honor to be even a small part of someone coming to faith in Jesus. We need to take this responsibility seriously and work diligently for the Gospel in all we do.

Reflections

_____

_____

_____

_____

_____

_____

Prayers

_____

_____

_____

_____

_____

_____

Saint Frances of Rome

Serving God doesn't always come at the cost of forsaking the desires of our hearts. Oftentimes, God plants these dreams within us for a reason. He loves to take our passions and turn them into something influential for His Kingdom! It's important to consider how the things you want most in life could serve the cause of the Gospel.

Saint Frances of Rome desired to be a wife and mother but also part of a religious order. She followed her dream of being a wife and mother until she was widowed after 40 years of marriage. God then lead her to the ordered life of a religious, even though she was not part of a convent. She devoted her life to fasting, prayer, service to others, and the reading of God's Word.

She was an excellent example of how our dreams can fit into God's bigger picture. The Lord planted both of those desires in her because He intended for them both to come to fruition.

She became a faithful wife who raised godly children and then served God by ministering to the needy. She didn't end up having to choose one or the other.

Psalm 37:4 reads:
"Take delight in the LORD, and he will give you the desires of your heart"
(NIV)

Even when you don't see a way for your heart's desires to come true, trust in God's plan. He can make anything happen and likely put those things on your heart because they're part of His plan.

Reflections

Prayers

Blessed Elias del Socorro Nieves

There will be times in your spiritual journey when it seems like everything is working against you. Satan loves to throw roadblocks on our path, trying to halt the spread of the Gospel. But God is mightier than the enemy's plans, inspiring His children to persevere through persecution and carry out His will no matter what they face.

Blessed Elias del Socorro Nieves was the prime example of perseverance. He beat the odds as an infant when he was not expected to survive after being born. At the age of twelve, he fought off death yet again after a struggle with TB. He went on to serve the Lord as the parochial vicar of the village of La Canada de Caracheo, Mexico, but the roadblocks on his path persisted.

In those times, the government was persecuting the church. He was forced to carry out his ministry hiding in the hills near the city. This less than ideal situation did not stop him from serving his people. Ultimately, he was martyred for his faith but left a legacy of perseverance that has inspired countless Christians since.

Hebrews 12:1 reads:
"Since we are surrounded by such a great cloud of witnesses, let us throw off everything that hinders and the sin that so easily entangles. And let us run with perseverance the race marked out for us" (NIV).

The example of Bless Elias del Socorro Nieves and all of the martyrs can motivate us to grow in perseverance. We must always look towards their examples when faced with our most challenging trials.

Reflections

_____

_____

_____

_____

_____

_____

_____

Prayers

_____

_____

_____

_____

_____

_____

_____

Saint Theresa of Calcutta

It's incredible what we can accomplish for the Kingdom when we partner with God in our lives. We are capable of so much more than we could ever know. The Lord has a way of revealing our inner strengths and gifts like nothing else can. When we live in a close relationship with Him, He shows us what we are to do and where we are to do it. When we follow Him with complete trust, amazing things happen.

Saint Theresa of Calcutta proved that massive impact could stem from the most humble of beginnings. As a young nun, she followed her calling from the Lord to establish the Missionaries of Charity and serve "the poorest of the poor." She obtained Indian citizenship and did basic medical training before working in the slums of Calcutta. Alongside Hilary Clinton, she set up a center in Washington DC for orphaned babies.

The order she founded has grown immeasurably, now consisting of nearly 5000 sisters worldwide who run homes for people who are dying, organizing mobile clinics, counseling programs, soup kitchens, orphanages, and schools. The influence of her work for the Lord is still felt by many today. She has left a lasting legacy on the world, all because of her obedience in following God.

In John 14:12, Jesus said:
"Very truly I tell you, whoever believes in me will do the works I have been doing, and they will do even greater things than these because I am going to the Father" (NIV).

Never forget the power you receive when you follow Jesus and your ability to win hearts for the Kingdom. It's a responsibility that we must never take lightly.

Reflections

Prayers

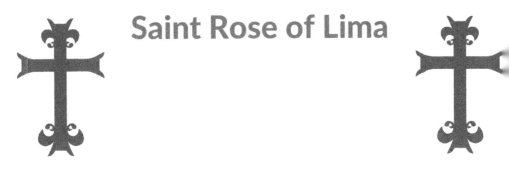

Saint Rose of Lima

As God's children, while we live in the world, we are not of the world. Our eternal home is in heaven, while our time here in Creation is but temporary. Striving towards a healthy spiritual life trumps worldly pleasures, and we must always keep our priorities straight. If we do, we will be better prepared for our eternal existence at the side of our Lord.

Saint Rose of Lima paved the way for us in demonstrating devotion to the pursuit of spiritual awareness. Despite her great beauty and the admiration of many men, she chose to live a life devoted to God instead. She even cut her hair and neglected her looks in order to detract those who were interested in her romantically.

As a saint, Rose of Lima was designated as a co-patroness of the Philippines and Saint Pudentiana; both saints were moved to second-class patronage in September 1942 by Pope Pius XII, but Rose remains the primary patroness of Peru and the local people of Latin America. Her image is featured on the highest denomination banknote of Peru.

1 Timothy 4:8 reads:
"For physical training is of some value, but godliness has value for all things, holding promise for both the present life and the life to come"
(NIV)

Strive always to deepen your spiritual awareness and relationship with God. There is nothing more vital that you can be doing in your life. Our lives here on Earth are temporary, but we will have eternity with the Lord forever.

Reflections

_____
_____
_____
_____
_____
_____
_____

Prayers

_____
_____
_____
_____
_____
_____

Blessed Giacomo Cusmano

God cares deeply for the plight of the poor in the world. He desires for all of His children to have access to everything that they need to live. It breaks His heart to see those He loves suffering and struggling to survive. We must emulate Him and find empathy in our hearts for our fellow human beings who are in desperate need.

Blessed Giacomo Cusmano displayed his heart for the poor from a young age. He lost his mother at just three years of age, but he was a religious child who was eager for education despite his hardship. His concern for the poor was so great that his family had to lock away his clothes, or little Giacomo would take them and give them all away to the poor.

We must be wise with our resources and seek ways in which we can alleviate the needy in our communities. Everything that we have is a gift from God, so we must be good and responsible stewards with all that He has entrusted us with. In doing so, we honor Him.

Psalm 83:3-4 reads:
"Defend the weak and the fatherless; uphold the cause of the poor and the oppressed. Rescue the weak and the needy; deliver them from the hand of the wicked" (NIV).

Concern for the poor is not a suggestion but a commandment from the Lord Himself. We must follow it with all of our hearts, spreading God's love to those we serve. When we do this, we are the hands of feet of Jesus.

Reflections

_____
_____
_____
_____
_____
_____
_____

Prayers

_____
_____
_____
_____
_____
_____
_____

Saint Agatha of Sicily

We need the strength that only God can provide when facing the most grueling trials of our lives. When our own courage is not enough to make it through what we are experiencing, God steps in and provides the help that we need. There are times in life that are so terribly we can do nothing but rely on Him. We must trust that He will be faithful and true, no matter what.

Saint Agatha of Sicily is perhaps our most incredible illustration of relying solely on God's courage and strength. After rejecting the advances of the Roman prefect Quintianus because of her vow to virginity and devotion to the Lord, she was subject to unexplainable torture and was eventually martyred. One of the trials she endured was the cutting off of her breasts with pincers.

In the midst of her pain, she prayed to God the following prayer: "Jesus Christ, Lord of all, you see my heart, you know my desires. Possess all that I am. I am your sheep: make me worthy to overcome the devil." Her example of courage and trust in the Lord is unparalleled and worthy of our admiration. She is the patron saint of breast cancer patients.

Never forget that no trial you ever face is too powerful for God to help you overcome. When it is all over, He will welcome you into His loving arms for eternity.

Revelation 21:4 tells us that
"He will wipe every tear from their eyes. There will be no more death or mourning or crying or pain, for the old order of things has passed away"
(NIV)

When struggling against your greatest pain, physical or mental, keep these immensely powerful words close to your heart.

Reflections

Prayers

Saint John de Brebeuf

Sometimes, it can seem that even when we have the best intentions that everything possible is standing in our way. We eagerly want to serve the Lord, but some enormous roadblock is standing in our way. In those times, it may seem impossible to clear such a hurdle, but rest assured that anything is possible with God. If He has called you to it, He will see you through it.

Saint John de Brebeuf felt the calling on his life from a very early age to enter the priesthood. He struggled to fulfill his calling because of his poor health. This obstacle ultimately did not deter him, though. At age 32, he was sent as a missionary to frontier Canada because the climate agreed with him and made him strong.

He struggled to learn the Huron language, but his determination won out. He stuck with it, knowing the importance of his task, and God saw it through. Saint John de Brebeuf completed his work, writing a catechism in the Huron language. His perseverance and trust in God's calling brought the church's teachings to an entirely new people group.

Romans 5:3-4 reads:
"but we also glory in our sufferings, because we know that suffering produces perseverance; perseverance, character; and character, hope"
(NIV)

Even when it seems like the world is standing in your way, let nothing pull you off of the path that God has laid before you. He will take your struggles and make them work for you, not against you. God will help you complete the amazing work that He has called you to do.

Reflections

_____
_____
_____
_____
_____
_____

Prayers

_____
_____
_____
_____
_____
_____

Saint Patrick

Though it may not seem like it, sometimes even the people who seem furthest away from God are only a step away from a life of faith. We often avoid those who consider themselves atheists because we believe that we stand no chance of reaching them in ministry. That is far from the truth. We should never let an opportunity to share the faith with anyone pass us by. We must be bold in our witness to the Gospel.

Saint Patrick reached many for the Gospel. He is the patron Saint of Ireland, even though he was born British. At the age of sixteen, he was kidnapped by pirates and found himself looking after pigs in Ireland.

After six years, he escaped and returned to England. There, he received a vision from God and went back to Ireland to follow his calling to serve as a missionary. Ireland was deeply entrenched in paganism at the time. Even in the midst of such a challenging place to preach the Gospel, he converted many souls to Christianity.

Matthew 28:19 reads:
"Go therefore and make disciples of all the nations, baptizing them in the name of the Father and the Son and the Holy Spirit" (NIV).

There will be times and places where this commandment will be challenging to follow. Nonetheless, we must trust in God to see our work to fruition. Ancestors in the faith such as Saint Patrick have proven to us that God comes through when we need Him most.

Reflections

Prayers

Saint Cyril of Jerusalem

Our understanding of Christian theology stems from a long tradition of Saints who studied tirelessly to explain the faith to others and to set a standard to defend against false teachings. Church tradition has brought so many layers of meaning from the Scriptures to our worldview and has united the body of Christ in thought. We are blessed by their teachings every day.

Saint Cyril of Jerusalem cared deeply for the catechisms of the church and devoted his life to Christian doctrine. He was known to teach for three hours every day during lent, going through the doctrine and creed step by step. He was a reliable and faithful servant of the Lord, eager to serve the people God had entrusted to him.

He wrote many documents that are essential to understanding the theology of the church. Most of his writings center on the instruction of catechisms and the order of the Liturgy. His influence on church tradition continues to live on to this day. His teachings are valued as some of the most influential in church history.

2 Timothy 3:16 reads:
"All Scripture is God-breathed and is useful for teaching, rebuking, correcting and training in righteousness" (NIV).

Saint Cyril of Jerusalem lived out this truth, showing how practical and vital that God's Word is to the church. His impact on how the church has engaged in worship over its history is undeniable. His devotion to the Bible stands as the standard set for us all.

Reflections

Prayers

Saint Joseph, Husband of Mary

Sometimes situations in our lives may not always be what they appear to be on the surface. God is often at work on a much deeper level that we cannot see. This reality is why living our lives by faith is so critical. We need God to guide us through every situation in life, especially those we don't understand.

Saint Joseph, the husband of Mary, came to one of those circumstances in life. The woman he was engaged to, Mary, suddenly became pregnant through no action of his own. He eas confused, and rightfully so. If faced with a similar situation, any one of us would assume the worst. Without God, there was no other possible reason behind what had happened.

Matthew 1:19 reads:
"Because Joseph her husband was faithful to the law, and yet did not want to expose her to public disgrace, he had in mind to divorce her quietly" (NIV).

Joseph's desire to protect Mary despite his understanding of the situation showed his great character. But there was something beyond surface-level that he just couldn't see. God was at work in the biggest way possible.

Joseph was faithful when God's messenger revealed the truth of the situation to him. He trusted in the Lord and took Mary as his wife. He was blessed with the honor of raising Jesus. Joseph is the Patron Saint of a Happy Death because he died with Christ and Mary on either side of him. We can all look towards his outstanding character and trust in God.

Reflections

Prayers

Saint Nicolas of Flue

Jeremiah 29:11

For I know the plans I have for you, declares the Lord, plans for welfare and not for evil, to give you a future and a hope. (ESV).

God calls us all to a different way of life. Some are lead to living in the world, working within society to influence for the Gospel. God sends others to work primarily within the church, shepherding and cultivating the faith of His people. Others yet are called to withdraw from the world, living the life of a hermit. The wisdom of such Saints is beyond compare, building up many Christians throughout church history.

Saint Nicholas of Flue committed to a hermit's life in the Ranft Valley of Switzerland, following a vision from God. He assisted at Mass daily, then spent the rest of the day in prayer. God granted him the gifts of prophecy and inedia, surviving for 19 years just on Holy Communion.

His way of life attracted spiritual students. In 1481 he was also able to be a mediator in a dispute that threatened civil war in Switzerland. His work in that role stopped the conflict, bring peace back to the people. His particular way of life didn't stop him from contributing to the world around him and bring up others in the faith.

No matter where God has called you, follow Him, even if it's to a way of life that society doesn't understand. There's no telling how He will impact the world through you. You can be the catalyst to real change in society if only you trust and walk with Him. Be open to anything that He asks of you, knowing that He has what's best for you in mind.

Reflections

Prayers

Blessed Clemens August von Galen

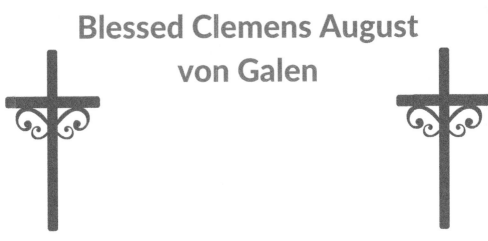

The courage that God grants us is unparalleled. There will be times in life where we will have to face something that is bigger than anything we'd imagine we'd have to deal with. It can be intimidating, no doubt, but we must ask God for the courage to stand up for what is right. Our willingness to advocate for the truth has the ability to shape history.

Blessed Clemens August von Galen found the courage through his faith to stand up to the Nazi regime. Most people would cower before such a force, but Blessed Clemens August von Galen knew that they had to be stopped. He fought bravely to end the Nazi program of euthanasia, the murdering of the old, crippled, and ill.

Joshua 1:9 reads:

"Have I not commanded you? Be strong and courageous! Do not tremble or be dismayed, for the Lord your God is with you wherever you go" (NIV).

We have no reason to fear because the all-powerful God who created the universe and everything that we know has got our back. Nothing that we face is bigger or stronger than Him.

With God on our side, there's nothing that can stand against us. We can rise up, standing firm as an advocate for the truth even in the darkest of situations. Be ready to accept the courage that God desires to give you when He calls you into action. He will fill you with bravery, unlike anything you have ever known.

Reflections

Prayers

Saint Turibius of Mogrovejo

God loves to use people who others would dismiss as agents of His great work. We see it throughout the Scriptures. The twelve disciples were made up of fishermen, a tax-collector, and others who were low on society's totem pole. God chose Moses to liberate the Israelites from bondage even though he had a speech impediment. God does amazing things through everyone that He calls. It doesn't matter how others view them; God sees them as valuable.

In 1575, Saint Turibius of Mogrovejo was selected by the King of Spain to serve as the Bishop of Lima even though he wasn't even a priest at the time! The Pope approved the decision, and Saint Turibius was subsequently appointed. He devoted himself entirely to his new role, baptizing and confirming over half a million souls.

Romans 15:7 reads:
"Accept one another, then, just as Christ accepted you, in order to bring praise to God" (NIV).

Never deny someone the opportunity to live out their calling just because their qualifications don't meet the requirements. Look at their heart, their calling, and their eagerness to serve the Lord. Just because somebody doesn't have a college degree or decades of experience doesn't mean that they shouldn't be living out the work that God has called them to do.

Remember, too, God's great mercy on you. He offered up His very own Son so that you may have eternal life.

That sacrifice extends to all. Everybody has a place in God's Kingdom and deserved to be treated as equal as part of the body of Christ. Let us never forget the importance of being humble as God's children.

Reflections

Prayers

Saints Perpetua and Felicity

Sometimes our faith calls us to great sacrifice. We live in the midst of a fallen world, where the enemy seeks to overthrow God's reign. Satan will confront us with the direst of circumstances in an effort to get us to renounce our faith. No matter what may become of us, we must never give in. The Lord Jesus Christ willingly sacrificed Himself to save us, so we must be willing to make any sacrifice for Him.

Saints Perpetua and Felicity are honored within church tradition for their willingness to give their life for Jesus just as He had done for them. They refused to renounce their faith, instead choosing to meet the furiosity of a mad cow and the cold steel of a gladiator's blade. The Roman arena was a cold and cruel place, but they'd rather face it than renounce their Lord. May their memory live forever.

In the Gospel of Matthew, Jesus warns us of such things:

"Blessed are ye, when men shall revile you, and persecute you, and shall say all manner of evil against you falsely, for my sake. Rejoice, and be exceeding glad: for great is your reward in heaven: for so persecuted they the prophets which were before you" (Matt. 5:11-12, NIV).

Though the age of martyrs seems like it's in the past, a brief glimpse at world news will show us that terrible things are still happening to Christians around the world today.

Both of these women were mothers who loved their children, just like so many of us today. We must remember their selfless devotion and pray that God would grant us similar strength today.

Reflections

Prayers

Saint Padre Prio

Though the miraculous occurrences found in Scripture may seem very distant from the world we live in today, we must remember that God has not stopped working in the world. God still performs miracles! The Spirit of God is still doing incredible things through many believers worldwide; we have just become too blind to see it. God's Kingdom has broken in on Earth and will continue to grow until its day of ultimate realization in the end times.

Saint Padre Pio is a 20th example of God working miracles through believers. Padre Pio was an Italian priest who was known for his piety and charity. He had the gift of the stigmata. He could see guardian angels, and he spoke with Jesus and the Virgin Mary. He was said to levitate and could perform miracles. The wisdom he left us is simple but profound: He famously advised, "Pray, hope, and don't worry."

1 Corinthians 12:28 reads:
"God has placed in the church first of all apostles, second prophets, third teachers, then miracles, then gifts of healing, of helping, of guidance, and of different kinds of tongues" (NIV).

The Bible makes it clear that the body of Christ holds immense power that God has shared with them so that they can carry out His will.

Don't disregard the spiritual gifts of others as religious fanaticism. Likewise, don't hesitate to cultivate the spiritual gifts that God has blessed you with. Be open-minded, willing to see God at work through everyone and everything. If you do, you are only limiting your God-given potential.

Reflections

Prayers

Saint Dulce of the Poor

We never know how the small seeds we plant can grow. What may seem like small, close-reaching work today may influence millions tomorrow. God's plan is larger than we can comprehend, and even the shortest steps of obedience can lead us on a grand journey. We must eagerly respond to every call that He places on our lives.

Dulce Pontes began her ministry caring for the poor who came to the convent's chicken yard in Salvador, Bahia, seeking her help. That former chicken yeard is not the site of the Santo Antonio Hospital, where more than 3000 people arrive each day for free medical treatment. The lasting impact of her work speaks for itself. What started as her helping those directly in front of her has exploded into one of Brazil's largest and most respected philanthropic organizations.

Philippians 1:6 reads:
"being confident of this, that he who began a good work in you will carry it on to completion until the day of Christ Jesus" (NIV).

God had begun a good work in Dulce Pontes, carrying it through to completion with the impact we see it having today. God desires to do the same thing in you! Wherever He is leading you today will have lasting reach beyond your wildest imagination.

Resist the urge to ever see your work in ministry as insignificant, even if it has started small. We can never comprehend the scope of God's plan. All we can do is trust Him in our obedience, knowing that He works through people like you and me.

Reflections

Prayers

Saint John of Lycopolis

God can provide unmatched spiritual preparation for ministry to those who seek it. We can read all of the books and pursue all of the degrees that we wish, but nothing replaces a since and intimate relationship with God if we want to become ministers of the Word. God is also available to us for prayer, meditation, and wisdom. All we must do is spend that time with Him.

Saint John of Lycopolis was an incredible example of this. Living on a mountain near Lycopolis, Egypt, he spent his time in prayer and meditation five days a week. The other days, he served the sick male students who sought him out for spiritual direction. The need became so great that he built a hospice for them.

Through his devout spiritual preparation, he received the gifts of prophecy, healing, and knowing his patients' hidden sins. God prepared him for ministry because Saint John of Lycopolis spent the time necessary with God. He developed a deep relationship with His Lord that equipped him to serve the numerous people that God sent his way.

How can you spend more time with God, and how will He equip you for ministry? These are important questions to consider as you continue along your spiritual journey.

Revelation 3:20 reads:
"Behold, I stand at the door and knock. If anyone hears my voice and opens the door, I will come in to him and eat with him, and he with me"
(NIV)

God desires to spend time with you today. How will you respond?

Reflections

Prayers

Saint Gianna Beterra Molla

James 4:17

So whoever knows the right thing to do and fails to do it, for him it is sin.
(ESV)

When our conscience aligns with God's teachings, it's essential to follow it no matter the cost. There will be times in life when what we know is right based on the things God has taught us is tested. The world will question us, making it easy to doubt our faith. But we must hold firm in our dedication to the Lord and doing what is right.

Saint Gianna Beterra Molla was an Italian Roman Catholic pediatrician While pregnant with her fourth child, she refused both an abortion and a hysterectomy despite knowing that this could result in her own death, which later occurred. Her medical career was in line with the Catholic Church's teachings, and she resolved to follow her conscience while helping others who needed her. In 2004, Gianna's husband and their children were present at her canonization. It was the first time that a husband had ever witnessed his wife's canonization.

I'm sure that Gianna's decision was criticized harshly by those around her, especially as she was part of the medical community. There must have been many who did not understand her selfless devotion to her decision. But through this decision, she did what was right and inspired countless people. Though facing considerable loss, I'm sure her family stood proud at her canonization, knowing full well the impact and weight of her sacrifice.

Never be willing to bend on something that you know is right. Our lives here on Earth are temporary, but eternity waits in God's presence. If we faithfully live out our lives here on Earth in relationship with God and in line with His ways, we will never face death, mourning, or pain again.

Reflections

_____

_____

_____

_____

_____

_____

_____

Prayers

_____

_____

_____

_____

_____

_____

Blessed Bertold of Mt. Carmel

As we journey through life, sometimes we find that the path we thought was right is not where we are supposed to be. We have to switch directions and make a bold change in our life. This situation can be trying, as we have devoted so much time and effort to what we were doing. But we must always be willing to be obedient to God's lead nonetheless because the rewards of following Him far outweigh the struggles.

Bertold was a soldier who fought in the Crusades. Following a vision of Christ, Bertold renounced his military life and became a hermit on Mount Carmel, taking his inspiration from Elijah the Prophet. His reputation for holiness spread, and other hermits moved to the area, including Saint Brocard. The community resulted in the founding of the Carmelites order.

The vision that Bertold received from God altered his path. He no longer lived a soldier's life but did a complete 180, living the life of a hermit devoted to the Lord instead. Though challenging to switch his path, His eager obedience to the Lord resulted in powerful results for God's Kingdom. An entire monastic order that has done marvelous deeds for the Kingdom arose because of him.

Don't cling more tightly to the path you are on today than to your faith in the Lord. If He calls you elsewhere, thank Him for the time you had where you are now, and move on to where He has shown you. Your obedience to Him could change the world, all for the sake of God's coming Kingdom.

Romans 11:29

For the gifts and the calling of God are irrevocable. (ESV).

Reflections

Prayers

Blessed Mary Restituta Kafka

Joshua 1:9

Have I not commanded you? Be strong and courageous. Do not be frightened, and do not be dismayed, for the Lord your God is with you wherever you go." (ESV).

Jesus paid the ultimate price so that we would have eternal life with God. There was no sacrifice too great for Him to make in service to the Lord. We owe everything we have to Him. There is no other way to salvation except through accepting Jesus Christ as our Lord and Savior. He paved the way for us all. We likewise must be willing to give it all for our faith. If we do, we will reap eternal rewards.

In 1914, Blessed Mary Restituta Kafka Joined the Franciscan Sisters of Christian Charity. Working as a surgical nurse, she was known as a protector of the poor and oppressed. Mary was a vocal opponent of the Nazis. She hung a crucifix in every room of a new hospital wing. The Nazis ordered them to be removed, but Mary refused.

She was arrested by the Gestapo and sentenced to death. It was decided that her execution would provide "effective intimidation" for others. She spent her remaining time in prison, caring for the other prisoners. She was offered her freedom if she would abandon her religious community, but she declined and was beheaded.

What are you willing to sacrifice for your faith? Are you truly ready to follow in Jesus' footsteps? The path of faith is not easy. It is filled with many trials, but we can find much inspiration in the fact that Jesus paved the way for us, defeating sin and death for us so that we could live in freedom with Him.

Reflections

_____
_____
_____
_____
_____
_____

Prayers

_____
_____
_____
_____
_____
_____

Saint Marguerite Bays

God is the great deliverer. There are times in life when we are afflicted with something that is beyond our power to overcome. God has the ability to reach into that situation and bring us healing. There have been countless stories over the years of people who have been miraculously healed by God from injuries, illness, other ailments, both physical and mental. God is remarkable in His power.

Saint Marguerite developed intestinal cancer and asked for the intercession of the Blessed Virgin Mary. She was miraculously healed. Following the healing, each Friday, Marguerite would undergo a period of paralysis and relive the Passion of Jesus. She received the gift of stigmata.

She devoted her life to caring for the people of her parish, including the sick, children, young women, and the poor of her community. God's deliverance played a critical role in her life, allowing her to serve as an inspiration to others in ways she was never capable of before.

Psalm 68:20 reads,:
"God is to us a God of deliverances; And to God, the Lord belong escapes from death" (NIV).

God desires to free us from our pain. Our most significant trials in life can turn into our most extraordinary testimonies. Just as those healed by Christ couldn't help but proclaim all the He had done for them, we likewise must share with others the things that God has delivered us from. If we do, we will convert many souls to Christianity. Their eternal salvation can be influenced by your choice to share or not share your testimony. Choose wisely!

Reflections

Prayers

Saint Ludovico Pavoni

Romans 12:6

Having gifts that differ according to the grace given to us, let us use them if prophecy, in proportion to our faith (ESV).

The purpose that God brings to our life has an impact on the world tha reaches past our mortal lifespan. Things that He has us do today car change the lives of people far into the future. We will never actually witness all that our work in ministry accomplishes, but we can res assured that God will use our purpose for great things.

Saint Ludovico Pavoni was the founder of an orphanage and associated trade school for teaching, printing, and publishing in Brescia, Italy. In 1823, Ludivico established The Publishing House of the Institute of Saint Barnabas. It still exists today but is now called Ancora. The school began taking in deaf and mute students. He founded an order of priests and brothers to run the school.

God is still using this work that Saint Ludovico Pavoni started long ago to further the cause of the Gospel. Just because Saint Ludovico Pavoni is no longer with us doesn't mean that his work passed with him. His influence lives on, reaching many for the faith. God be praised for the way that He works in the world, allowing us to leave our mark here in Creation on the hearts of others.

We are truly Christ's hands and feet. This is an astounding truth and one we should carry with us always. Emulating the lives of the saints has benefits for our life now, the lives of others, and for eternity to come. Let us strive towards their examples with eagerness and faithfulness.

Reflections

Prayers

Blessed Maria Teresa Casini

We live in a time where it's easy for us to make excuses to avoid doing the things that we know we should be doing. There are more distractions around us than ever before, pulling our eyes away from our true goal. Our troubles in this world are also abounding, attempting to hamper our goals. The faith of others can serve to inspire us to overcome these obstacles in our lives, no matter what form they come in.

Blessed Maria Teresa Casini lived the final year of her life paralyzed. For many, this would mark the end of their missional work and service to others. But Maria, armed with faith and devotion, never stopped working towards the purpose to which she had been called. She ran her ministry from bed, meeting, teaching, and counseling sisters, priests, and seminarians until the end.

She was the founder of the Victims of the Sacred Heart, who continue to do their good works for the Lord to this day. Their main goal is to assist and support priests and other vocations worldwide. Maria had the desire to support priests so that the Lord had an adequate supply of suitable priests for the ministry.

What things in life are holding you back from continuing to do what you know deep down you are supposed to be doing? Ask God to help you overcome these obstacles.

Let Philippians 4:13 become the motto by which you live your life:
"I can do all this through him who gives me strength" (NIV).

Reflections

Prayers

Saint Isidore

Today, we have the internet. It can be a great tool to help us in our ministry. The resources available there are instant and unlike anything we've ever had access to before. We also have the ability to connect with others worldwide more conveniently than ever. The ability to collaborate with other believers anywhere and reach others for the Gospel is unlike any other time previously in history. We must be good stewards of this gift that God has blessed us with.

Saint Isidore is known as the "Patron Saint of the Internet." He gained this moniker from Pope Daint John Paul II himself because his mind was known to be a vast storehouse of knowledge. Saint Isidore used his education and wisdom to a significant effect to evangelize many.

We, too, must strive towards knowledge of our faith, its history, and God's Word itself. Having a healthy understanding of these things helps us to be more well-rounded people of faith. The knowledge of God's Word particularly assists us in living out the lives that being a Christian demand of us. Not gaining insight into the intricacies of our faith leaves us vulnerable to backsliding and false teachings.

Proverbs 1:7 reminds us that
"The fear of the LORD is the beginning of knowledge; fools despise wisdom and instruction" (NIV).

God's ways are different than the ways of the world, and we must be diligent in both learning them and applying them to our lives. In doing so, we will please our Heavenly Father.

Reflections

Prayers

Saint Vincent Ferrer

Proverbs 3 5:6

Trust in the Lord with all your heart, and do not lean on your own understanding. In all your ways acknowledge him, and he will make straight your paths.(ESV).

God's ways are mysterious, and some people have his anointing hand on their lives from the very beginning. From day one, their lives impact those around them for the Gospel in profound ways. God's plan is perfect, and He has deemed these people to be critical parts of His goal to bring as many to salvation as possible. We must strive to follow their examples in every way possible.

Saint Vincent Ferrer was one such person. Before he was born, his father was told in a dream that his son would be famous throughout the world. His mother gave birth to him with no pain whatsoever. This miraculous start to his life was just the start of what God had planned for him.

Vincent spent most of his life as an itinerant preacher on the highways and byways of Spain, France, and Italy, drawing enormous crowds and inspiring them to a deeper life in Christ. He had the gift of tongues. He slept on the floor, fasted endlessly, performed many miracles, and converted thousands of people to Christ.

Has God yet revealed His glorious plan for your life? Never forget that you were created with a purpose. Even though some spend their whole lives walking in their purpose, it is never too late to start. If God has revealed His purpose for you, start walking in it today. If He has not, ask Him humbly in prayer to show you what He would have you do so, you can get started right away.

Reflections

Prayers

Saint John Baptist de la Salle

Educators have a special role in our society. The work that they do i essential to the health of our communities. They work tirelessly to invest in the education of our children for their future. Those we teach us in the church are to be praised as well, instilling in us godly wisdom that will serve us our entire lives.

Saint John Baptist de la Salle was a lifelong educator. He was approached by other men wanting to be teachers, so he founded the Order of Christian Brothers. He inherited a fortune from his parents and decided to donate it to the poor rather than open new schools. His legacy is still active today in numerous countries where over a thousand educational institutions still operate in his name.

Proverbs 18:15 reads:
"The heart of the discerning acquires knowledge, for the ears of the wise seek it out" (NIV).

We should never forget the value of learning in our lives. There should never come a time when we don't seek to understand more about God and our faith.

Through prayer, reading the Bible, and fellowship with others, we must always seek additional wisdom in our lives. The benefits of God's wisdom will carry us through everything that we encounter in life. God longs to teach us always, revealing secret knowledge to us that we would never learn elsewhere. We must make spending time with Him and seeking His wisdom a priority above all.

Reflections

_____
_____
_____
_____
_____
_____

Prayers

_____
_____
_____
_____
_____
_____

Saint Peter

Inevitably, we will all make mistakes in life. There is no avoiding this truth. We are not expected to be perfect, but that's why Jesus came and lived the perfect life in place of us. God will forgive us always if only we come to Him and repent. There's nothing in the world that can separate us from God's love. Jesus brings healing and redemption to sinners, allowing them to move past their mistakes and grow into the people that God has called them to be.

Saint Peter learned this profound lesson. He loved Jesus but made a grave mistake. After the Last Supper, Peter denied Jesus three times. After Jesus' resurrection, Jesus offered Peter forgiveness and gave him three chances to affirm his love again. Peter powerfully responded to Jesus' forgiveness, becoming the first Pope and doing precious work to establish the church in the world.

Peter was martyred in Rome. In 1950, bones were discovered beneath the altar of Saint Peter's Basilica. Pope Paul VI announced that these remains were likely to belong to Saint Peter.

John 13:37 reads:
"Peter said to Him, 'Lord, why can I not follow You right now? I will lay down my life for You'" (NIV).

Peter was zealous for the Lord and a prime example of the eagerness that we should have within ourselves to serve Christ.

Don't let any mistakes that you have made in life discourage you from serving the Lord. Just like Peter, Jesus will give you forgiveness if you come to Him with repentance and the genuine desire to serve Him.

Reflections

Prayers

Saint Faustina

Some believers have the spiritual gift of seeing visions. These visions inspire great devotion in the receiver and those they are shared with. The retelling of these visions serves as a powerful testimony to God and the way that He works in our lives. One of the most well-known of these visions is known as the Divine Mercy.

Saint Faustina's apparitions of Jesus Christ inspired the Roman Catholic devotion to the Divine Mercy. She had visions and conversations with Jesus, which she wrote about in her diary. She produced an image of her vision in accordance with Christ's wishes. Jesus told her that he wanted the Divine Mercy image to be "solemnly blessed on the first Sunday after Easter.

While the concept of seeing visions may seem strange to some, there is biblical evidence for such events.

Joel 2:28 reads:
"I will pour out my Spirit on all people. Your sons and daughters will prophesy, your old men will dream dreams, your young men will see visions" (NIV).

The Bible makes it clear that the spiritual gift of seeing visions is valid and authentic.

If you have this spiritual gift, be bold in proclaiming the messages that God imparts to you. If you do not possess this gift, be open to those that do. Never dismiss another's genuine desire to share with you what God has revealed to them. Remember Saint Faustina's incredible example of how the visions some receive from the Lord can develop powerful devotion in others.

Reflections

_____

_____

_____

_____

_____

_____

Prayers

_____

_____

_____

_____

_____

_____

Saint Stanislaus

John 5:24

Truly, truly, I say to you, whoever hears my word and believes him who sent me has eternal life. He does not come into judgment, but has passed from death to life. (ESV).

Throughout history, many have lost their lives in defense of the faith. All kinds of people and groups over the years have attacked the faith in many ways. With great courage and strength derived from God, many warriors of the faith had stood tall to repel these attacks. We must remember them gratefully and be thankful for their boldness so that we can continue to experience the church as we know it today.

Saint Stanislaus was the Bishop of Krakow, Poland. Still, he had many disputes with Poland's King Bolesław II. Stanislaus excommunicated Bolesław. When the King entered Krakow's Cathedral for Mass, the service was immediately stopped due to his excommunication. Bolesław was furious and wanted Stanislaus killed, but the assassins refused, so the King had to enter the chapel where Stanislaus was saying Mass and killing him himself.

Saint Stanislaus stood up for the church and his faith. Even with the threat of violence, he didn't hesitate to lay down his life for the Gospel as Jesus did for him. In this, he has lead many by example. We must put our faith above all, remembering that life here on Earth is temporary but what lies after with God is eternal through Jesus Christ.

Never mistake the importance of eternity. The comforts of life are fleeting, but the pleasures of heaven never fade. The things we experience here will pass, but we will live in God's Kingdom by Jesus' side forever. Keep your eyes focused on an eternal perspective always.

Reflections

Prayers

Saint Thomas of Canterbury

Matthew 18:20

For where two or three are gathered in my name, there am I among them.
(ESV)

Throughout history, the dynamic between church and state hasn' always been so amicable as it is in the West in recent times. There have been many points over time, even in certain parts of the world today where the government of a particular persecutes the church. It's a sad day when officials of a region won't support and encourage the great work that the church does in their community or nation.

Saint Thomas of Canterbury found himself embroiled in the midst of one of these times. Henry II, King of England, used his power to deny the church of its rights and privileges. Thomas Becket was the Archbishop of Canterbury from 1162 until his murder in 1170. He was in conflict with Henry II, the King of England, over the Church's rights and privileges. He was murdered by followers of the King in Canterbury Cathedral. He is venerated as a saint and martyr by both the Catholic Church and the Anglican Communion.

We are blessed to live in a time where this issue is less prevalent. For many of us, we've never even considered encountering such a situation. The church is always available and safe to go to for most of us. We must be grateful to live in a time and place where persecution of the church is not so evident in our everyday lives.

Let this truth serve as motivation to attend church regularly. The opportunity to go safely is something that many believers have not been so blessed to have over the years. Don't neglect meeting with the body of Christ and to worship the Lord together.

Reflections

_____
_____
_____
_____
_____
_____
_____

Prayers

_____
_____
_____
_____
_____
_____
_____

Reflections

Prayers

Reflections

_____

_____

_____

_____

_____

_____

Prayers

_____

_____

_____

_____

_____

_____

Made in the USA
Coppell, TX
19 February 2023

13094875R00050